Contents

Introduction

What this book contains	3
How to set, mark and interpret the tests	3
Helping your child sit tests	4
What to do with the results	5

English

Testing your child's English	6
Reading tests	8
Writing tests	21
Spelling and handwriting test	24
Answers	26

Mathematics

Testing your child's mathematics	35
Test 1 (Level 3)	36
Test 2 (Level 4)	40
Test 3 (Level 5)	45
Answers	50

Science

Testing your child's science	52
Science test	53
Answers	62

Text © ST(P), David Evans, Sean McArdle and Wendy Wren 1997

The right of ST(P), David Evans, Sean McArdle and Wendy Wren to be identified as the authors of this work has been asserted by them in accordance with the Copyright, Designs and Patents Act 1988.

All rights reserved. The copyright holders authorise ONLY users of *More Practice Papers for the Key Stage 2 National Tests* to make photocopies or stencil duplicates of page 32 for their own immediate use. No other rights are granted without permission in writing from the publishers or under licence from the Copyright Licensing Agency Limited. Further details of such licences (for reprographic reproduction) may be obtained from the Copyright Licensing Agency Limited of 90 Tottenham Court Road, London W1P 9HE. Copy by any other means or for any other purpose is strictly prohibited without prior written consent from the copyright holders. Application for such permission should be addressed to the publishers.

First published in 1997 by
Stanley Thornes (Publishers) Ltd
Ellenborough House
Wellington Street
CHELTENHAM GL50 1YW

97 98 99 00 / 10 9 8 7 6 5 4 3

A catalogue record for this book is available from the British Library.

ISBN 0 7487 3070 2

Designed by Ian Foulis & Associates, Saltash, Cornwall

Printed and bound in Great Britain by The Baskerville Press, Salisbury, Wiltshire

Introduction

What this book contains

During your child's last year in primary school (Year 6) he or she will sit Key Stage 2 National Assessment Tests in the three core subjects: English, mathematics and science. These tests take place in school over a period of about a week during May and the results are reported back to you and are also passed on to the secondary school your child will attend. For each of the three subjects your child will be given a mark in the form of a level. Most children will perform in the range of Levels 3–5 by the end of Key Stage 2 with an average performance being roughly Level 4.

The tests are a valuable measure of your child's performance in school. Not only will they be influential in the secondary school's initial assessment, they may also be your child's first experience of sitting formal written tests. It is extremely helpful if that first experience can be a positive one, and many parents and children have found the practice material in the first book of *Practice Papers for the Key Stage 2 National Tests* to be an invaluable resource.

This second book provides you with a further complete set of practice papers for each of the three subjects, with the principle aim of preparing your child confidently for the tests. Each set of papers will:

- provide test questions similar to those in the National Tests for Levels 3–5 of the National Curriculum.

- give your child practice in sitting the tests: working to a set time, getting familiar with the format and style of the tests and developing effective test strategies.

- give you a broad guide to your child's likely level of performance within Levels 3–5 of each subject.

- give you an idea of strengths and weaknesses in your child's learning.

How to set, mark and interpret the tests

The tests for the three subjects require different lengths of time to complete. The shortest is science (35 minutes); English and mathematics each have up to three papers which require about $2\frac{1}{4}$ hours. In school such papers will be set over a period of about a week. At home, in order to keep the process relaxed, you will probably want to spread the papers over a longer period.

Each set of papers allows you to set, mark and level your child's work in the subjects without any prior knowledge of the National Curriculum. First read the detailed advice on setting the papers; then set the test. When your child has finished each paper use the answers to mark it. Enter the number of marks gained on the papers as shown on the next page.

Add up the marks on each page and enter them at the foot of the page. Add the marks for all the pages to find the total mark obtained, then use the conversion box at the end of the answers to get an idea of National Curriculum level.

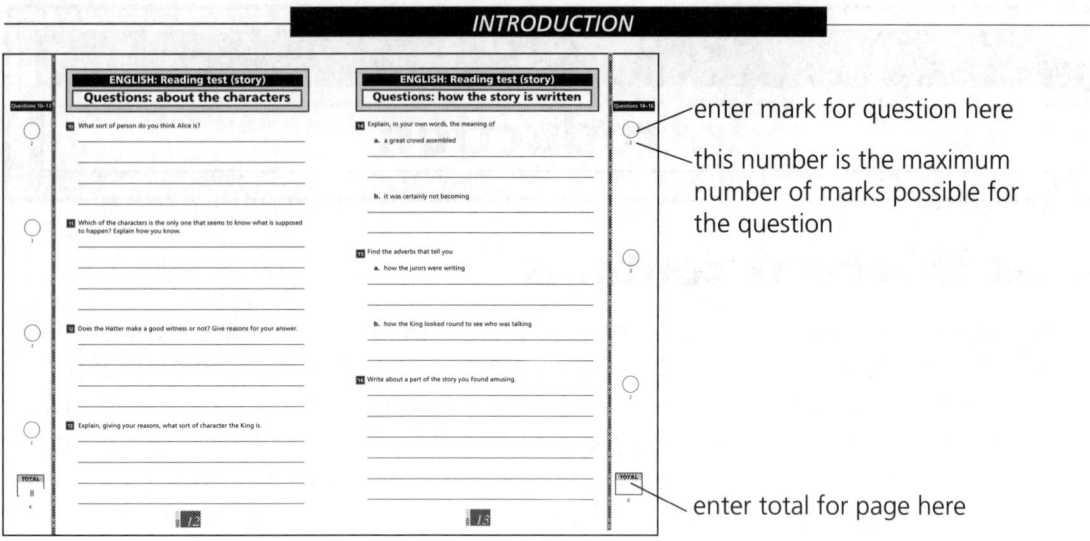

- enter mark for question here
- this number is the maximum number of marks possible for the question
- enter total for page here

Helping your child sit tests

As well as practising the content of the tests, one of the key aims of this book is to give your child practice in working under test conditions. All the tests are timed and your child should try to complete each one within the given time. In order to make best use of the tests, and to ensure that the experience is a positive one for your child, it is helpful to follow a few basic principles:

- Talk with your child first before embarking on the tests. Present the activity positively and reassuringly. Encourage your child to view doing the papers as an enjoyable activity which will help, always making him or her feel secure about the process.

- Ensure that your child is relaxed and rested before doing a test. It may be better to do a paper at the weekend or during the holidays rather than straight after a day at school.

- Ensure a quiet place, free from noise or disturbance, for doing the tests.

- Ensure that there is a watch or clock available.

- Ensure that your child understands exactly what to do for each paper and give some basic test strategies for tackling the task. For example:

  - Try to tackle all the questions but don't worry if you can't do some. Put a pencil mark by any you can't do, leave them and come back at the end.

  - Make sure you read the questions carefully.

  - Go straight on to the next page when each is finished.

  - Try to pace yourself over the allowed time. Look over the whole paper first to get an idea of how many questions there are. Don't spend too long over one question.

  - Use all your time.

  - If you have any time over at the end go back over your answers. This is particularly important if you are doing one big piece of work, such as writing a story.

INTRODUCTION

- Taking the time to talk over a test beforehand and to discuss any difficulties afterwards will really help your child to gain confidence in the business of sitting tests.

- However your child does, ensure that you give plenty of praise for effort.

What to do with the results

The tests in this book and the results gained from them are only a guide to your child's likely level of performance. They are not an absolute guarantee of how your child will actually perform in the National Tests themselves. However, these papers will at least allow your child to get practice in sitting tests; they will also give *you* an insight into the strengths and weaknesses in their learning.

If there are particular areas of performance which seem weaker, it may be worth providing more practice of the skills required. It is also valuable to discuss any such weaknesses with your child's class teacher, and to seek confirmation of any problem areas and advice on how to proceed. It is always better to work in partnership with the school if you can. Above all ensure that you discuss these issues with your child in a positive and supportive way so that you have their co-operation in working together to improve learning.

ENGLISH
Testing your child's English

What do the National Tests cover?

At Key Stage 2 your child will be studying three areas of English in school. These are:

1. Speaking and Listening
2. Reading
3. Writing

The national tests cover only reading and writing and set three papers for Levels 3–5: Reading; Writing; Spelling and Handwriting.

We have provided papers for each of these three tests. You will find that the tests for English are slightly more intricate than those for the other subjects and each one is different in style. Instructions for setting each one are detailed below. After the tests have been done, you will have to add together the marks from each paper to gain an impression of your child's overall performance in English. This is explained in the Answers section on page 34.

Setting the reading test (time: 60 minutes)

1. The reading test involves reading and answering questions on:
   - a story
   - a poem
   - a piece of informational writing

   The aim of the assignment is to test children's ability to read, understand and respond to different types of writing. The national test does this as one paper and allows one hour for it. You can either set it as a complete paper or do each part separately. We suggest for ease of practice that you break the reading test into three short tests.

2. Set the story reading paper as follows:
   - You will find the story on pages 8–10. Allow your child ten minutes to read it through. Encourage them to read it carefully and more than once if there is time.
   - Your child now has to answer the twenty questions about the story on pages 10–14. Allow 20 minutes for this. The story can be referred back to whilst answering the questions. It may be helpful to jot notes on the story or to underline useful information. Before answering the questions ensure that the procedure is understood.
   - Questions 1 to 8 require one right answer to be ringed.
   - Question 9 requires ordering events in the story by numbering.
   - The remaining questions require written answers. Some require only one- or two-word answers, others will be more lengthy. This is not a test of spelling, punctuation or grammar but children should be as accurate as possible when answering.
   - Any questions which seem difficult to answer should be left and returned to at the end if time allows.

3. Set the poetry paper in a similar way:
   - Allow five minutes to read the poem on page 15 through carefully.
   - Allow ten minutes to answer the questions on pages 16 and 17. Refer back to the poem and jot notes around it if helpful.
   - Remind your child to answer as many as possible. Leave any questions that seem too difficult and come back to them at the end.

4. Set the information paper in a similar way:
   - Allow five minutes to read the piece on page 18 through carefully.
   - Allow ten minutes to answer the questions on pages 19 and 20. Refer back to the passage and jot notes around it if helpful.
   - Remind your child to leave and come back to any difficult questions.

Setting the writing test (time: 60 minutes)

1. The writing test involves writing either a story or a piece of non-narrative writing, such as a description or a letter. This book provides the option of writing a story or a letter. Talk to your child about which he or she would like to do. Explain that spelling, grammar and punctuation are important in this piece of work. Allow one hour for the test whichever option is chosen.

2. If your child wishes to write a letter for the test, proceed as follows:
   - The child will need to use the planning sheet on page 21 and the letter starting point on the top of page 23. Paper to write the letter on will also be required.
   - Start by explaining that you will read aloud the letter starting point and proceed to do so.
   - Now introduce the planning sheet and talk through with your child the various

6

headings. Your discussion should focus on the key features of a letter:

- The importance of being aware of the subject of the letter and the reason for writing it.
- The need to have a good opening to get the reader's attention.
- The need to keep the reader's attention throughout the piece of writing.
- The need to end in an appropriate way.
- The layout of letters and the right style for the reader. Remind your child that you use different tones to write to a bank and to write to a friend.

- Now tell your child that they have 15 minutes to make notes for the letter on the planning sheet. Remember that notes can be very short, maybe just a few words, to get the main ideas down.
- After 15 minutes it is time to write the letter. Give a short break if required. Forty-five minutes is given for writing the letter, using the planning sheet as a structure.
- Remind your child of the time and let them know when there are 15 minutes left. If the work is finished early encourage your child to reread it carefully, checking grammar, punctuation and spelling.

3 If your child wishes to write a story proceed as follows:

- They will need to use the planning sheet on page 22 and the story starting sheet at the bottom of page 23. Paper to write the story on will also be required.
- Start by explaining that there is a choice of two story starting points but that only one should be chosen. Read them both aloud and ask your child to choose one.
- Now introduce the planning sheet and talk through with your child the various headings. Your discussion should focus on the key features of a story:
  - the importance of establishing the setting and the plot of the story as quickly as possible;
  - the need to keep the number of characters manageable so that there is time to describe them adequately and make the reader feel that they know the characters through what they do and say;
  - the importance of a good strong opening to get the reader interested;
  - the need to continue the story in such a way that the reader 'needs to know' what is going to happen;
  - the importance of ending the story well and not leaving it hanging in mid air.
- Remind your child that this has to be a complete short story, and not an episode from a longer one.
- Now tell your child that they have 15 minutes to make notes for the story on the planning sheet. Remember that only one story starter can be chosen and its title should be written at the top. Remember that ideas can be in note form to save time.
- After 15 minutes it is time to write the story. Give a short break if required. Forty-five minutes is available for writing the story and the planning sheet should be used as a structure.
- Remind your child of the time and let them know when there is 15 minutes left. If the work is finished early encourage careful re-reading to check grammar, punctuation and spelling.

Setting the spelling and handwriting test (time: 15 minutes)

1 The spelling test

The spelling test is a short passage with words missed out that your child has to spell. Proceed as follows:

- Turn to page 24 and show your child the passage with the words missed out. On page 32 you will find a complete copy of the passage. You will need either to cut this out or to photocopy it.
- Read the complete passage aloud clearly while your child follows the incomplete one without writing anything.
- Explain that you are going to read the passage again slowly, whilst your child writes in the missing words as clearly as possible.
- Tell your child that if they are unsure of a spelling they should put the letters which they think are right.
- Now read the passage again slowly, pointing out the missing words and giving time to write the word on the appropriate line.
- Allow ten minutes for the whole test.

2 The handwriting test

- The handwriting test on page 25 is a short passage which follows on from the spelling test.
- Read your child the instructions which appear on the sheet above the passage to be copied.
- Allow five minutes for the handwriting test.

ENGLISH: Reading test (story)
Alice in Wonderland

Alice has followed a white rabbit down a hole to a very strange place indeed. After many adventures she finds herself in a courtroom just before a trial is about to begin.

The King and Queen of Hearts were seated on their throne when they arrived, with a great crowd assembled about them – all sorts of little birds and beasts, as well as the whole pack of cards. The Knave was standing before them, in chains, with a soldier on each side to guard him, and near the King was the White Rabbit, with a trumpet in one hand, and a scroll of parchment in the other. In the very middle of the court was a table with a large dish of tarts upon it. They looked so good that it made Alice quite hungry to look at them. 'I wish they'd get the trial done,' she thought, 'and hand round the refreshments!' But there seemed to be no chance of this so she began looking about her, to pass the time away.

Alice had never been in a court of justice before, but she had read about them in books, and she was quite pleased to find that she knew the name of nearly everything there. 'That's the judge,' she said to herself, 'because of his great wig.' The judge, by the way, was the King, and as he wore his crown over the wig, he did not look at all comfortable, and it was certainly not becoming.

'And that's the jury-box,' thought Alice, 'and those twelve creatures,' (she was obliged to say 'creatures' you see because some of them were animals, and some were birds,) 'I suppose they are the jurors.' She said this last word two or three times over to herself, being rather proud of it, for she thought, and rightly too, that very few little girls of her age knew the meaning of it at all. However, 'jurymen' would have done just as well.

The twelve jurors were all writing very busily on slates. 'What are they all doing?' Alice whispered to the Gryphon. 'They can't have anything to put down yet, before the trial's begun.'

'They're putting down their names,' the Gryphon whispered in reply, 'for fear they should forget them before the end of the trial.'

ENGLISH: READING TEST (STORY)

'Stupid things!' Alice began in a loud, indignant voice, but she stopped hastily, for the White Rabbit cried out, 'Silence in court!' and the King put on his spectacles and looked anxiously round to see who was talking.

Alice could see, as well as if she were looking over their shoulders, that all the jurors were writing down 'stupid things' on their slates. She could even make out that one of them didn't know how to spell 'stupid' and that he had to ask his neighbour to tell him. 'A nice muddle their slates will be in before the trial's over!' thought Alice ...

'Herald, read the accusation!' said the King. On this the White Rabbit blew three blasts on the trumpet, and then unrolled the parchment scroll and read as follows:

> 'The Queen of Hearts, she made some tarts,
> All on a summer day.
> The Knave of Hearts, he stole those tarts,
> And took them quite away!'

'Consider your verdict,' the King said to the jury. 'Not yet, not yet!' the Rabbit hastily interrupted. 'There's a great deal to come before that!'

'Call the first witness,' said the King, and the White Rabbit blew three blasts on the trumpet and called out, 'First witness!' The first witness was the Hatter. He came in with a teacup in one hand and a piece of bread-and-butter in the other.

'I beg pardon, your Majesty,' he began, 'for bringing these in but I hadn't quite finished my tea when I was sent for.'

'You ought to have finished,' said the King. 'When did you begin?' The Hatter looked at the March Hare, who had followed him into the court, arm-in-arm with the Dormouse.

'Fourteenth of March, I *think* it was,' he said.

'Fifteenth,' said the March Hare.

'Sixteenth,' added the Dormouse.

'Write that down,' the King said to the jury, and the jury eagerly wrote down all three dates on their slates, and then added them up and reduced the answer to shillings and pence. 'Take off your hat,' the King said to the Hatter.

'It isn't mine,' said the Hatter.

'Stolen!' the King exclaimed, turning to the jury who instantly made a memorandum of the fact.

'I keep them to sell,' the Hatter added as an explanation. 'I've none of my own. I'm a hatter.'

Here the Queen put on her spectacles and began staring hard at the Hatter who turned pale and fidgeted.

'Give your evidence,' said the King, 'and don't be nervous, or I'll have you executed on the spot.' This did not seem to encourage the witness at all. He kept shifting from one foot to the other, looking uneasily at the Queen, and in his confusion he bit a large piece out of his teacup instead of the bread-and-butter ...

ENGLISH: *Reading Test (story)*

'Give your evidence,' the King repeated angrily, 'or I'll have you executed whether you're nervous or not.'

'I'm a poor man, your Majesty,' the Hatter began in a trembling voice, 'and I hadn't begun my tea – not above a week or so – and what with the bread-and-butter getting so thin – and the twinkling of the tea ...'

'The twinkling of the *what*?' said the King.

'It began with the tea,' the Hatter replied.

'Of course twinkling begins with a T!' said the King sharply. 'Do you take me for a dunce? Go on!'

From *Alice in Wonderland* by Lewis Carroll

ENGLISH: Reading test (story)
Questions: about the story

Questions 1–9

1 The Knave was

| crying | in chains | on the throne | guarding the pack of cards |

2 The trumpet and the scroll of parchment were carried by

| the Knave | the Queen | the White Rabbit | the King |

3 On the table there was

| a dish of tarts | a chain | a pack of cards | a trumpet |

4 To pass the time away Alice

| ate a tart | blew the trumpet | looked around | spoke to the Gryphon |

TOTAL
4

ENGLISH: *Reading Test (story)*

5 The jurors were

| eating | talking | sleeping | writing |

6 The first witness was

| the White Rabbit | the Hatter | the Dormouse | the Queen |

7 The Hatter was carrying

| a cup and saucer | a scroll of parchment | a slate | some spectacles |

8 The King thought that the Hatter had

| made the hat | eaten the hat | stolen the hat | borrowed the hat |

9 Here are some things which happen in the story. Put them in the right order by numbering each line. The first sentence has been numbered for you.

_____ The Knave was accused of stealing the tarts.

1 _____ The Knave was in chains in the courtroom.

_____ The White Rabbit cried out, 'Silence in court.'

_____ He said that he hadn't finished his tea.

_____ The King thought the Hatter had stolen the hat.

_____ Alice looked around and saw the judge and jurors.

_____ The Hatter was called into the court room.

ENGLISH: Reading test (story)
Questions: about the characters

10 What sort of person do you think Alice is?

_____

_____

_____

_____

11 Which of the characters is the only one that seems to know what is supposed to happen? Explain how you know.

_____

_____

_____

_____

12 Does the Hatter make a good witness or not? Give reasons for your answer.

_____

_____

_____

_____

13 Explain, giving your reasons, what sort of character the King is.

_____

_____

ENGLISH: Reading test (story)
Questions: how the story is written

Questions 14–16

14 Explain, in your own words, the meaning of

    a. a great crowd assembled

    b. it was certainly not becoming

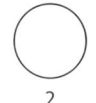

15 Find the adverbs that tell you

    a. how the jurors were writing

    b. how the King looked round to see who was talking

16 Write about a part of the story you found amusing.

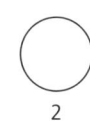

TOTAL

6

13

ENGLISH: Reading test (story)
Questions: your opinion

17 Did you enjoy reading this story?

Yes _____   No _____

Explain, giving your reasons, if you would like to read about what happens to the Knave or not.

_____
_____
_____

18 Explain, giving your reasons, why you think the jurors would, or would not have done a good job.

_____
_____
_____

19 Will the Knave have his head chopped off? Write about how you think the trial will end.

_____
_____
_____

20 Would you have liked to be in the court room that day?

Yes _____   No _____

Explain the reasons for your answer using parts of the story to help you.

_____
_____
_____

ENGLISH: Reading test (poetry)

The Loner

He leans against the playground wall,
Smacks his hands against the bricks
And other boredom-beating tricks,
Traces patterns with his feet,
Scuffs to make the tarmac squeak,
Back against the wall he stays –
And never plays.

The playground's quick with life,
The beat is strong.
Though sharp as a knife
Strife doesn't last long.
There is shouting, laughter, song,
And a place at the wall
For who won't belong.

We pass him running, skipping, walking,
In slow huddled groups, low talking.
Each in our familiar clique
We pass him by and never speak,
His loneness is his shell and shield
And neither he nor we will yield.

He wasn't there at the wall today,
Someone said he'd moved away
To another school and place
And on the wall where he used to lean
Someone had chalked
'watch this space'.

Julie Holder

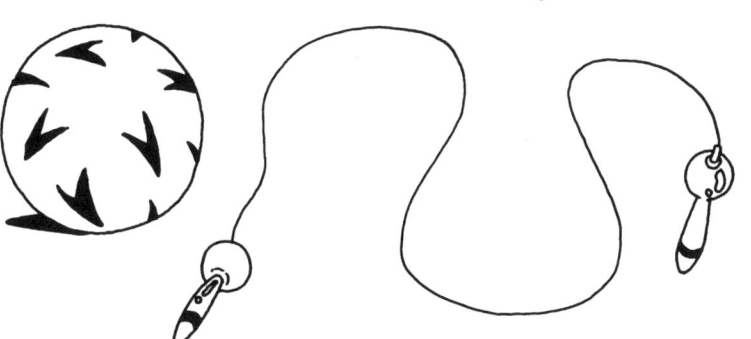

ENGLISH: Reading test (poetry)
Questions

1 The poem describes two very different types of people. Who are they?

_____

_____

_____

_____

2 What does the boy do as he stands against the wall?

_____

_____

_____

_____

3 What do the other children in the playground do?

_____

_____

_____

_____

ENGLISH: *READING TEST (POETRY)*

4 Imagine that you are the boy standing by the wall. Describe your thoughts and feelings.

_____

_____

_____

_____

_____

5 What is the poet suggesting might happen by saying that someone chalked 'watch this space' on the wall where the boy used to lean?

_____

_____

_____

_____

_____

6 Explain, giving your reasons, why you do or do not like this poem.

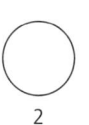

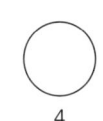

_____

_____

_____

_____

_____

_____

_____

_____

_____

ENGLISH: Reading test (information)
Argentina

Four hundred and fifty years ago Sebastian Cabot, an Italian working for the Spanish, explored a river in South America. He encountered friendly Indians who wore beautiful silver jewellery. He was convinced that he had discovered a land rich in silver and named the river Rio de la Plate – river of silver. The country around the river was later called Argentina – land of silver. These names remain to this day, although Cabot and his men were disappointed to find that the silver had come from what is now Peru some 1,000 miles away!

Argentina	
People:	Argentinians
Location:	Southern part of South America
Area:	1,068,297 square miles
Population:	Estimated at 32,000,000
Capital city:	Buenos Aires
Major language:	Spanish
Major religion:	Roman Catholic
Monetary unit:	Austral (1 austral = 100 centavos)
Chief products:	Agriculture: wheat, corn, barley, oats, rye, cotton, tobacco, oilseeds, sugarcane, grapes
Manufactured:	leather goods, petroleum products, wine, iron, paper, tobacco products
Mineral:	petroleum, coal, iron ore, tin, lead, zinc.

ENGLISH: Reading test (information)
Questions

1 What two things did Cabot notice about the Indians?

2

2 Why did he call the river Rio da la Plate?

2

3 What was the country around the river called and why?

2

4 Were the names given to the river and the land justified? Give your reasons.

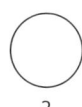
3

5 Why is the population of Argentina 'estimated'?

2

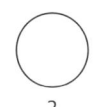
TOTAL

11

ENGLISH: READING TEST (INFORMATION)

6 Why do you think that

    a. the major religion is Catholic?

    b. the language is Spanish?

7 What is the more common name for 'petroleum'?

8 Explain, in your own words, what is meant by

    a. 'agriculture'

    b. 'manufactured'

    c. 'mineral'

9 This information is about Argentina. Where would you find similar information about other countries?

TOTAL

9

OVERALL SCORE

20

ENGLISH: Writing test
Letter planning sheet

How will you begin your letter if:

you know the person's name

_____

you do not know the person's name

_____

Are you writing the letter because:

you want to complain (what about?)

_____

you want information (what about?)

_____

you are pleased about something (what?)

_____

Make notes on what you will write in your letter.

_____

_____

_____

_____

How will you end your letter if:

you know the person's name

_____

you do not know the person's name

_____

ENGLISH: Writing test
Story planning sheet

Title
_____

Setting

where does your story take place?

_____

when does it happen?

_____

Characters

who are they?

_____

what do they look like?

_____

what sort of people/animals are they?

_____

Opening

how will you begin your story?

_____

Middle

what happens in your story?

_____

End

how will you finish your story?

_____

ENGLISH: Writing test
Letter starting point

Stuck for stickers!

You and all your friends are collecting sports stickers to fill a sporting sticker book. Your local shop used to sell the stickers but has now stopped. It is very difficult for you to get the stickers from anywhere else.

Write a letter to persuade the shop owner to sell the stickers again. Give as many reasons as you can why it would be good for you and your friends, and good for the shop.

OVERALL SCORE

20

ENGLISH: Writing test
Story starting point

Choose **one** of these starting points for your story.

1 Write a short story with the title *'The night the snow came'*.

2 Write a short story which opens with the sentence *'Everything had been going very well until we heard the knock at the door.'*

OVERALL SCORE

20

ENGLISH: Spelling and handwriting test
David Livingstone

1 David Livingstone grew up in the _little_ Scottish village of Blantyre. At the _end_ of each long working day he found _time_ to go to evening _classes_ and spent most of his money on _books_. He was _particually_ interested in other countries and nature. He read for hours and soon had a good general _knowlage_. He studied _medician_ and decided to go to Africa to _heal_ people and to tell them about God.

In 1840 David Livingstone landed on the _coast_ of Africa, the country in which he was to _spend_ most of his _life_. He worked, at first, in Kuruman _with_ Dr Moffat. He had to _travel_ hundreds of miles _through_ unexplored _terrortry_. He married Dr Moffat's _Daughter_ and they went two hundred miles further _north_ to continue their _work_. They had _four_ children so Mrs Livingstone left her _husband_ to return to _England_. He went on to explore Africa without his _family_.

David Livingstone had many _adventures_. On one occasion, he was in great _danger_ as a _lion_ _charged_ him. It broke his arm before his men _managed_ to kill it.

Some years later he returned to _Britian_ where he _recieved_ a hero's welcome.

OVERALL SCORE

30

24

ENGLISH: SPELLING AND HANDWRITING TEST

2 Here is a short passage which gives more information about David Livingstone. Write it out below very neatly in your own handwriting. Remember to make your writing as neat as possible, joining your letters if you can.

David Livingstone went to Africa three times and reported on the wonders of Victoria Falls and the Kalahari Desert. He died there in 1873 but his body was brought back to England and he was buried in Westminster Abbey.

David Livingstone went to Africa three times and reported on the wonders of Victoria Falls and the Kalahari Desert. He died there in 1873 but his body was brought back to England and he was buried in Westminster Abbey.

OVERALL SCORE

ENGLISH: Answers
Reading tests

To gain an impression of your child's performance in English you will have to add together the marks from each paper. You will find this explained in detail on page 34.

Story

1 The Knave was in chains. — *1 mark*

2 The White Rabbit carried the trumpet and the scroll. — *1 mark*

3 A dish of tarts was on the table. — *1 mark*

4 Alice looked around to pass the time away. — *1 mark*

5 The jurors were writing. — *1 mark*

6 The first witness was the Hatter. — *1 mark*

7 The Hatter was carrying a cup and saucer. — *1 mark*

8 The King thought the Hatter had stolen the hat. — *1 mark*

9
  1. The Knave was in chains in the court room.
  2. Alice looked around and saw the judge and the jurors.
  3. The White Rabbit cried out, 'Silence in court.'
  4. The Knave was accused of stealing the tarts.
  5. The Hatter was called into court.
  6. He said that he hadn't finished his tea.
  7. The King thought the Hatter had stolen the hat. — *7 marks*

10 Alice appears to think a lot of herself. She is clever and is quick to see how stupid others are. — *2 marks*

11 The White Rabbit. He has to tell the King that they are not ready for the verdict yet. — *2 marks*

12 No. He talks only about himself and the reader gets the feeling that he doesn't know anything about the tarts. — *2 marks*

13 The King can be described as fierce/bossy/forgetful. — *2 marks*

14
  a. many people (creatures) have gathered — *1 mark*
  b. it didn't suit him/he didn't look good in it — *1 mark*

14
  a. busily/eagerly — *1 mark*
  b. anxiously — *1 mark*

16 Award up to 2 marks for a clear description of an amusing incident in the passage. — *2 marks*

17 Award no marks for 'Yes' or 'No'. Award up to 3 marks for the reasons given. — *3 marks*

18 The jurors are unlikely to do a good job as they seem to write everything down, do sums, find difficulty in spelling and generally do not know what is going on. — *3 marks*

ENGLISH: Answers

19 Award 1 mark for a clear description of how the trial will end. Award another 1 mark if the pupil has suggested that the trial will probably never reach any conclusion as it seems such a muddle. *2 marks*

20 Award no marks for 'Yes' or 'No'. Award up to three marks for reasons supported by parts of the story. *3 marks*

Poetry

1 The type of people who like to be in a crowd and the type of people who find it difficult to mix with others. *2 marks*

2 He hits the wall and makes his shoes squeak on the tarmac. *1 mark*
He tries to overcome the feeling of boredom. *1 mark*

3 The other children shout, laugh, sing, run, skip walk, talk. *2 marks*
They quarrel but it never lasts for very long. *1 mark*

4 Lonely *1 mark*
Award an extra mark for an answer which shows insight into the fact that either he may want to be alone or he may want to join in but finds it too difficult. *1 mark*

5 That there will be someone else to fill the space as there are always people who won't or can't join in. *2 marks*

6 A child will score no marks for simply stating that he/she does or does not like the poem or writes 'I don't like poems about school'. Marks should be awarded where reasons specific to the poem are given. *4 marks*

Information

1 They were friendly and they wore silver jewellery. *2 marks*

2 He thought he had found the source of silver. *2 marks*

3 He called the country Argentina which means land of silver. *2 marks*

4 No they were not justified because the silver came from Peru. *3 marks*

5 The population is 'estimated' because no one can be sure exactly what the population is. *2 marks*

6 a. The country was first visited and colonised by countries whose religion was Catholic. *1 mark*
b. Cabot was working for the Spanish when he found the land. *1 mark*

7 Petrol *2 marks*

8 a. agriculture – farming crops and animals *1 mark*
b. manufactured – things which are made *1 mark*
c. mineral – rocks, gems etc. found in the ground *1 mark*

9 An encyclopaedia/reference book *2 marks*

ENGLISH ANSWERS
Writing tests

In order to get an idea of your child's level in writing you will need to assess the writing under three headings:

1. Purpose and organisation
2. Grammar
3. Styles

Children do not develop at the same rate across these three areas so dividing up the marks in this way allows you to see your child's strengths and weaknesses. Marking writing requires you to make judgements about the quality of the writing rather than just ticking right and wrong answers. Guidance for deciding your child's level performance against the three headings is given below. Once you have decided which level description best fits your child's work for each heading award the number of marks shown for that level. Add together the marks they have gained under each heading to get an overall score for writing.

Story writing

Purpose and organisation

What you are looking at under this heading is the content of the story.

Level 2

Look for:
- A clear opening to the story. Your child may use story language such as 'One day', 'Once upon a time', 'It was Sunday and ...'.
- Two or more events in sequence. At this level the events will be little more than a list of what happens. They will not be described in detail.
- Character(s) will be introduced. Your child will probably only give the name of the character(s) and you will not feel you know either what they look like or their personality.

Marking: 4 marks

Level 3

Look for:
- A simple but appropriate ending. This gives evidence that your child has thought through where the story is going. Inappropriate endings which often occur include 'And then I woke up', 'And then I died'!
- A setting for the story. Your child will begin to give details of where the story takes place. Some description such as 'It was dark in the wood ...', 'The snow covered the trees ...'.
- More detailed description of character. This includes a physical description of the character(s) such as 'Jane was tall and had red hair ...'. Also how the character(s) might be feeling, 'He was sad because he had lost his football ...'.
- How will the reader react? Your child will have some idea of what they want their story to 'feel' like. As the reader are you amused, frightened, unhappy?

Marking: 6 marks

ENGLISH: ANSWERS

Level 4

Look for:

- Paragraphs. Your child will have used paragraph divisions to separate the beginning and/or ending from the rest of the story. The correct form of paragraphing is by indenting on a new line, but simply beginning a new line or missing a line is acceptable at this level.

- Events are logically related. The events of the story will be more detailed and should follow on from one another logically. Your child will not have assumed that you know something has happened.

- Beginning, middle and end. As a reader you will begin to get the feeling that the story has a beginning, middle and end. It is not rambling and inconclusive.

- Interaction between characters. The characters in the story should relate to one another. If one character is hurt, another character should react appropriately, e.g. showing concern. If one character tells a joke, another character may laugh or say 'I've heard that one before'.

- Developing character. As the reader you should begin to feel you are getting to know the characters through what your child tells you about them, through what they say or through what other characters say about them.

Marking: 8 marks

Level 5

Look for:

- Paragraphs. Your child should be using paragraphs in the body of the story for such things as a new event, a change of scene, introduction of a new character etc.

- Events. Your child may attempt to introduce a second set of events such as a flashback where the writer or one of the characters relates events that have happened earlier which have a bearing on the story.

- Beginning. The opening of the story will be convincing and your child may have experimented by starting with dialogue, or by having a mysterious opening, the details of which are revealed as the story progresses.

- Middle. The body of the story will have elements of dialogue, action and description.

- End. The end convincingly relates to the body of the story. This may neatly tie up the loose ends or deliberately leave the reader guessing.

- The writer in control. Your child will have developed a point of view known as a 'narrative voice'. This takes the form of comments on the action, 'Now Sally should not have opened that door ...', or indications of characters' thoughts and feelings, 'Ben felt a chill of fear ...'.

Marking: 10 marks

Grammar

What you are looking for under this heading is the correct use of punctuation, capital letters, tenses and pronouns.

Styles

What you are looking for under this heading are sentence structure connectives and vocabulary.

Level 2

Look for:

- Sentences. At least two sentences where capital letters are used at the beginning and a full stop or question mark is used at the end.

Marking: 2 marks

Look for:

- Spoken language structures. Your child will write in much the same way as she/he would tell you the story.

- Connectives. Use of simple connectives to link ideas, 'and', and 'so', and 'then'.

- Vocabulary. The words your child uses will be very general: 'She had to get the bus' rather than 'She had to catch the bus'; 'Someone came into the room' rather than 'The old man came into the room'. Other examples of this general vocabulary include make, do, have, go, thing, something.

Marking: 2 marks

ENGLISH: ANSWERS

Grammar (continued)   Styles (continued)

Level 3

Look for:

- Sentences. At least half the sentences on the first page should begin with a capital letter and end with a full stop or question mark.

Marking: 3 marks

Look for:

- Written language structures. Your child will begin to use sentences structures which are appropriate to written rather than spoken language.
- Connectives. These should be used to show contrast, 'but'; connection in time, 'when', 'also'; and explanation, 'so', 'because'.
- Vocabulary. Your child will be using vocabulary to give more detail, 'a blue book', 'one frosty morning', 'he ran quickly', 'she soon went to sleep'.

Marking: 3 marks

Level 4

Look for:

- Sentences. At least three-quarters of the sentences on the first page should begin with a capital letter and end with a full stop or question mark.
- Commas. Commas should be used to separate items on a list: 'The boy bought apples, pears, oranges and bananas'.
- Speech. If speech is included then speech marks should signal the beginning and ending of the spoken words in at least half of the instances.
- Question marks and exclamation marks. By this level, these should generally be used correctly.
- Tenses. Your child's writing should not wander from past to present tense or vice versa: 'Jim walked along the path. He runs across the road'.
- Pronouns. These should be consistent. Children often slip from the third person into the first person and back again, 'She was very happy. I had won the race and she got a prize'.

Marking: 4 marks

Look for:

- Written language structures. Your child should increasingly write in ways that do not rely on the way she/he would speak:

  Spoken structure: 'They're really dreading going to the dentist.'

  Written structure: 'The twins were not looking forward to their visit to the dentist.'

- Connectives. Using connectives to help order ideas and give emphasis, 'if', 'when', etc.
- Vocabulary. You will feel that your child's vocabulary has been chosen with some care to add detail and interest to the story, 'a large, dirty machine', 'a strong, howling wind'.

Marking: 4 marks

Level 5

Look for the following on the first page:

- Sentences. There should be no more than two mistakes in sentence punctuation.
- Commas. As well as for lists, commas should be used for parts of sentences, 'She rushed into the house, falling over the broken chair'.
- Speech. Speech marks and the comma to introduce/conclude direct speech should be correct in three-quarters of the instances used, 'I don't want to go,' he said. He said, 'I don't want to go.'
- Question marks and exclamation marks. These should be used correctly.

Marking: 5 marks

Look for:

- Written language structures. Your child will be using a variety of sentence constructions, 'He walked to the door ...', 'Walking to the door ...', 'As he walked to the door ...'.
- Connectives. Using connectives to refer back, 'I went to the shop that I had been to before ...' and to avoid repetition, 'The book was on the table and it was open at the first page ...'.
- Vocabulary. Your child will be using varied and appropriate vocabulary to give interest and detail to the story.

Marking: 5 marks

ENGLISH: ANSWERS

Letter writing

Purpose and organisation

What you are looking for under this heading are the form and content of the letter.

Level 2

Look for:
- Form. Your child will have a grasp of a simple letter format.
- Content. There will be some relevant points but they will not be developed or connected.
- Reader's knowledge. Your child will assume you know about the issues and not give full explanations or information.

Marking: 4 marks

Level 3

Look for:
- Form. A more secure grasp of the form of a letter.
- Content. There should be an introductory statement and some sensible connection between the points covered.
- Reader's knowledge. The letter will give more information and your child will have included details to add interest.

Marking: 6 marks

Level 4

Look for:
- Form. Most of the appropriate conventions of letter writing will be in place and your child should begin to separate the points by means of paragraphing.
- Content. There will be a relevant introduction, the main points clearly covered and the letter will end in a conclusive way, rather be left 'hanging in mid-air'.
- Reader's knowledge. The purpose of the letter will be clear and the information/ background that the reader needs will, for the most part, be included.

Marking: 8 marks

Level 5

Look for:
- Form. The appropriate conventions of letter writing will be in place.
- Content. There will be good coverage of the main points linked by such phrases as, first of all, for instance, another problem.
- Reader's knowledge. Your child will have used the introduction to set out clearly the purpose of the letter and the conclusion to, sum up, appeal to the reader, suggest a course of action.

Marking: 10 marks

Grammar

What you are looking for under this heading is the correct use of punctuation, capital letters, tenses and pronouns.

Level 2

Look for:
- Sentences. At least two sentences where capital letters are used at the beginning and a full stop or question mark at the end.

Marking: 2 marks

Level 3

Look for:
- Sentences. At least half the sentences on the first page should begin with a capital letter and end with a full stop or question mark.

Marking: 3 marks

ENGLISH: ANSWERS

Grammar (continued)

Level 4

Look for:
- Sentences. At least three-quarters of the sentences on the first page should begin with a capital letter and end with a full stop or question mark.
- Commas. Commas should be used to separate items on a list and in the address, greeting and signature.
- Question marks and exclamation marks. By this level, these should generally be used correctly.
- Tenses. Your child's writing should not wander from the past to present tense and vice versa, 'I was shocked at the state of your shop I am visiting yesterday'.
- Pronouns. These should be consistent. Children often slip from the third person into the first person and back again, 'She went in to the shop yesterday and I was not happy with what I saw'.

Marking: 4 marks

Level 5

Look for the following on the first page:
- Sentences. There should be no more than two mistakes in sentence punctuation.
- Commas. Commas should be used to separate parts of sentences, 'I am writing to you in the hope that you can, if at all possible, meet me ...'.
- Question marks and exclamation marks. These should be used correctly.

Marking: 5 marks

Styles

The levels of attainment under this heading for letter writing are the same as those for story writing. Refer to the Styles section of the marking criteria for Story Writing (see pages 29–30).

ENGLISH ANSWERS
Spelling and handwriting tests

Spelling

David Livingstone grew up in the **little** Scottish village of Blantyre. At the **end** of each long working day he found **time** to go to evening **classes** and spent most of his money on **books**. He was **particularly** interested in other countries and nature. He read for hours and soon had a good general **knowledge**. He studied **medicine** and decided to go to Africa to **heal** people and to tell them about God.

In 1840 David Livingstone landed on the **coast** of Africa, the country in which he was to **spend** most of his **life**. He worked, at first, in Kuruman **with** Dr Moffat. He had to **travel** hundreds of miles **through** unexplored **territory**. He married Dr Moffat's **daughter** and they went two hundred miles further **north** to continue their **work**. They had **four** children so Mrs Livingstone left her **husband** to return to **England**. He went on to explore Africa without his **family**.

David Livingstone had many **adventures**. On one occasion, he was in great **danger** as a **lion charged** him. It broke his arm before his men **managed** to kill it.

Some years later he returned to **Britain** where he **received** a hero's welcome.

30 marks

ENGLISH: ANSWERS

Handwriting test

In order to get an idea of your child's level in handwriting you will need to decide which description and example best fits the sample of writing in the test. Award the number of marks shown for that level.

Level 2

Letters are not joined when writing.

A resistor is to make things high and low power. Like if you cut a pencil in half and clip the wires on to the pencil then

Marking: 3 marks

Level 3

There is the beginning of clear, legible writing, showing the ability to join letters.

The time machine whirred lights flashed across the transporter grid. They got brighter and brighter.

Marking: 4 marks

Level 4

The writing is more fluent and legible, showing the ability to join letters. Spaces between words will be regular, and the letters themselves of a similar size.

The time machine whirred. Lights flashed across the transporter grid. They got brighter and brighter. The

Marking: 5 marks

Level 5

The writing is clear, legible and neat in a joined-up (cursive) style.

The time machine whirred. Lights flashed across the transporter grid. They got brighter and brighter. The

Marking: 6 marks

ENGLISH ANSWERS
Finding a level for your child

The total number of marks a child could gain over the various elements of the English test are as follows:

Reading – (story)	40 marks
Reading – (information)	20 marks
Reading – (poetry)	15 marks
Writing (either story or letter)	20 marks
Spelling	30 marks
Handwriting	6 marks
Total	131 marks

One way of assessing your child's level is by adding the marks gained overall and using the table below:

Conversion of score into National Curriculum Levels

Level	Marks
Below Level 2	0 – 9
Level 2	10 – 33
Level 3	34 – 66
Level 4	67 – 98
Level 5	99 – 131

The table above is a somewhat simplistic indicator of level, as a child who did extremely well in, say, the reading test, but very badly in the spelling, could still gain an overall Level 4 mark whereas, in reality, the spelling in itself would have to improve for this to be reflected in the result of the overall national test.

A more sensible approach would be as follows:

If your child scores:

- up to a quarter of the marks for each individual test then grade the overall test as Level 2.
- between a quarter and a half of the marks for each individual test then grade the overall test as Level 3.
- between a half and three-quarters of the marks for each individual test then grade the overall test as Level 4.
- over three-quarters of the marks for each individual test then grade the overall test as Level 5.

MATHEMATICS
Testing your child's mathematics

What do the National Tests cover?

At Key Stage 2 your child will be studying four areas of mathematics in school. These are:

1. Using and Applying Mathematics
2. Number and Algebra
3. Shape, Space and Measures
4. Handling Data

The National Tests exclude Using and Applying Mathematics and concentrate on the other three areas: Number and Algebra; Shape, Space and Measures; Handling Data. Of these Number and Algebra is the most important and occupies the most space in the tests. For the tests in May your child will probably sit two papers. However, for ease and simplicity of marking we have presented the maths content in three papers which are explained below.

Setting the tests (time: 45 minutes each test)

1. The three tests need to be done in order. Test 1 covers Level 3, Test 2 covers Level 4 and Test 3 covers Level 5. Forty-five minutes should be allowed for each one.

2. Your child will need:
   - a pencil
   - a ruler
   - a calculator
   - tracing paper
   - a protractor

   It is suggested that you encourage your child just to cross out mistakes, rather than use a rubber.

3. Ensure that your child understands that they have to write answers on the blank lines. Sometimes boxes are provided which will ask your child to show how the answer has been worked out.

4. Explain the use of calculator symbols in the margin:

    means a calculator must be used.

    means a calculator may not be used.

   If no symbol appears, a calculator may be used if desired. However, from May 1996, pupils are not allowed to use calculators in one of the test papers. It would therefore be helpful for your child not to make too much use of a calculator in these papers.

5. If your child gets stuck on any question, encourage them to go on to the next one.

6. Because these tests are graded for difficulty your child will find each test harder than the one before. Explain to children that they are unlikely to complete all the questions in all three tests and to do their best. If your child struggles on one particular test it is probably not worth proceeding to the next one but ensure that you offer praise for what has been achieved. You can get a good idea of your child's overall level in mathematics even if they cannot proceed beyond Test 1.

7. As with all the tests, ensure your child goes back over answers if they finish early.

MATHEMATICS
Test 1

1 The number 163 can be made using the three cards.

[6] [1] [3]

   a. What is the largest number which can be made using the three cards? _____

   b. What is the smallest number which can be made using the three cards? _____

2 a. Match the numbers in figures on the left with the numbers in words on the right.

450	Five hundred and four
540	Four hundred and five
504	Five hundred and forty
405	Four hundred and fifty

   b. Which of the numbers is nearest to 500? _____

   c. Which of the numbers is 500 to the nearest 10? _____

   d. Which of the numbers is not in the 5 times table? _____

3 [639]   [567]   [240]

   a. Which of the numbers is larger than 567? _____

   b. Which of the numbers is less than 567? _____

   c. Write 240 in words. _____

TOTAL

MATHEMATICS: Test 1

1 Patrick buys three things in the shops. One costs £1.24, one costs £3.40 and one costs £2.75. Use a calculator to work out how much he spent altogether.

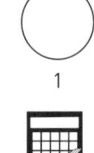

_____

2 These are the number of house points gained in one week.

	Chichester	Drake	Murray	Nelson
Year 3	25	42	31	40
Year 4	54	23	67	12
Year 5	31	29	26	36
Year 6	44	21	53	22

a. Which house had the highest points in Year 4? _____

b. Which house had the lowest score in Year 6? _____

c. Which year had the highest score in Nelson? _____

d. How many more points did Drake get than Chichester in Year 3?
_____

e. How many more points did Murray get than Nelson in Year 6?
_____

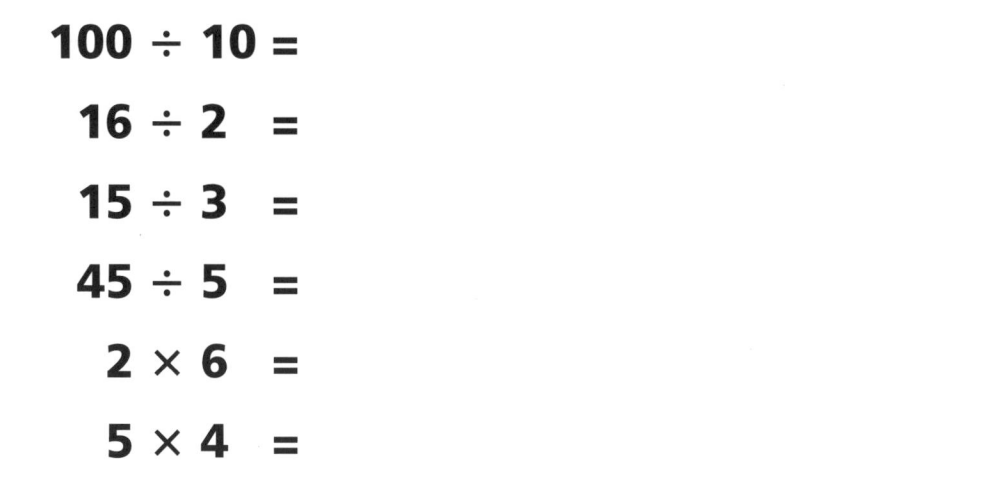

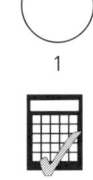

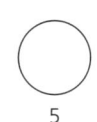

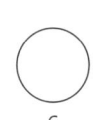

3 Join up the sum on the left with the answers on the right.

100 ÷ 10 =   9

16 ÷ 2 =   5

15 ÷ 3 =   20

45 ÷ 5 =   8

2 × 6 =   10

5 × 4 =   12

MATHEMATICS: Test 1

1.

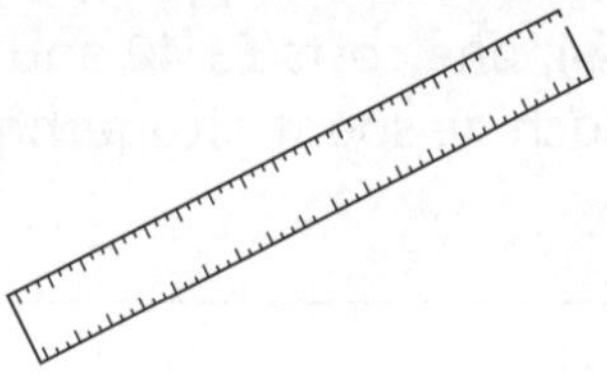

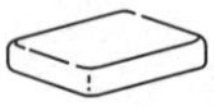

25 p   14 p   20 p   45 p

Use a calculator to work out each child's list.

    a. Kuldip buys a ruler, a pencil and a protractor. _____

    b. Sarah buys two pencils and a rubber. _____

    c. Amy buys a protractor, a rubber and a pencil. _____

    d. Anila buys one of each. _____

2. Join up the clocks on the left with the clocks on the right which say the same times.

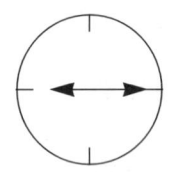

06:30

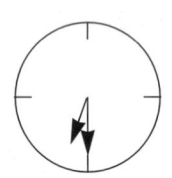

03:00

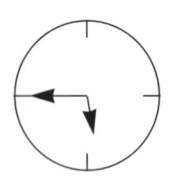

09:15

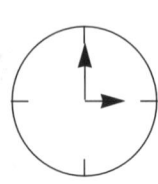

05:45

3. Write either 'centimetres' or 'metres' in the gaps so that the sentences will make sense.

    a. My hand is about 10 _____ long.

    b. The classroom is $4\frac{1}{2}$ _____ long.

    c. The child is 120 _____ tall.

    d. The football pitch is 45 _____ wide.

MATHEMATICS: Test 1

1 Fill in the missing numbers in the squares to make each sum correct.

    a. 4 × ☐ = 16   **b.** ☐ × 5 = 35

    c. ☐ × 9 = 90   **d.** 3 × ☐ = 15

2 Ali wants to sort shapes out into those with right angles and those without. Help him by putting these shapes in the right column.

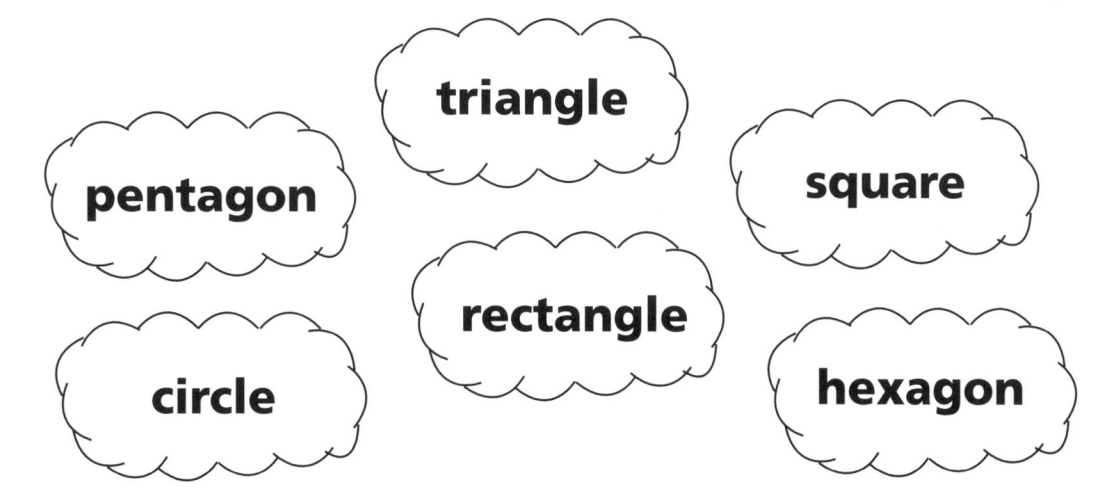

triangle

pentagon

square

rectangle

circle

hexagon

with right angles	without right angles

3 A triangle can be made by putting three matchsticks together.

    a. How many matchsticks would be needed to make

        a HEXAGON _____

        a PENTAGON _____.

    b. Two different shapes can be made using 4 matches. What are they?

        _____

MATHEMATICS
Test 2

1 Bricks are stacked in piles of 100
How many piles are there at each building site?

How many are left over?

Building site **A**   890 bricks = _____ piles

Building site **B**   1427 bricks = _____ piles

Building site **C**   2406 bricks = _____ piles

Building site **D**   4029 bricks = _____ piles

2 Fill in the numbers in the squares to make each sum correct:

a. 81 ÷ ☐ = 9   b. 49 ÷ ☐ = 7

c. 42 ÷ 6 = ☐   d. ☐ ÷ 5 = 9

3 Peter gets 15 correct spellings out of 20. Read the sentences and put a tick (✔) if it is correct or a cross (✗) if it is wrong.

a. Peter got $\frac{3}{4}$ correct ☐

b. Peter got less than 50% correct ☐

c. Peter got 25% wrong ☐

4 The factors of 6 are 1, 2, 3, and 6.
Write down all the factors of each number.

a. 8 → ☐ ☐ ☐ ☐

b. 16 → ☐ ☐ ☐ ☐ ☐

c. 49 → ☐ ☐ ☐

MATHEMATICS: Test 2

1 Samantha has three pieces of wood. Piece A is 1.34 m, Piece B is 1.27 m, Piece C is 1.26 m. She needs to put two pieces together to make a length of 2.53 m. Which pieces should she use?

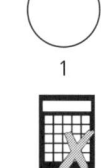

_____

2 Billy is not sure what a mirror line is and has drawn the other half of these shapes where he thinks they should be. Put a tick (✔) if he is right or a cross (✘) if he is wrong.

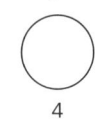

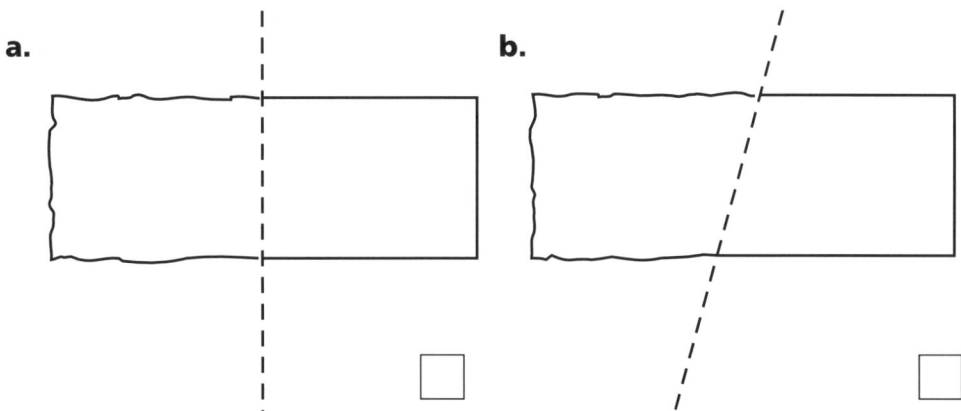

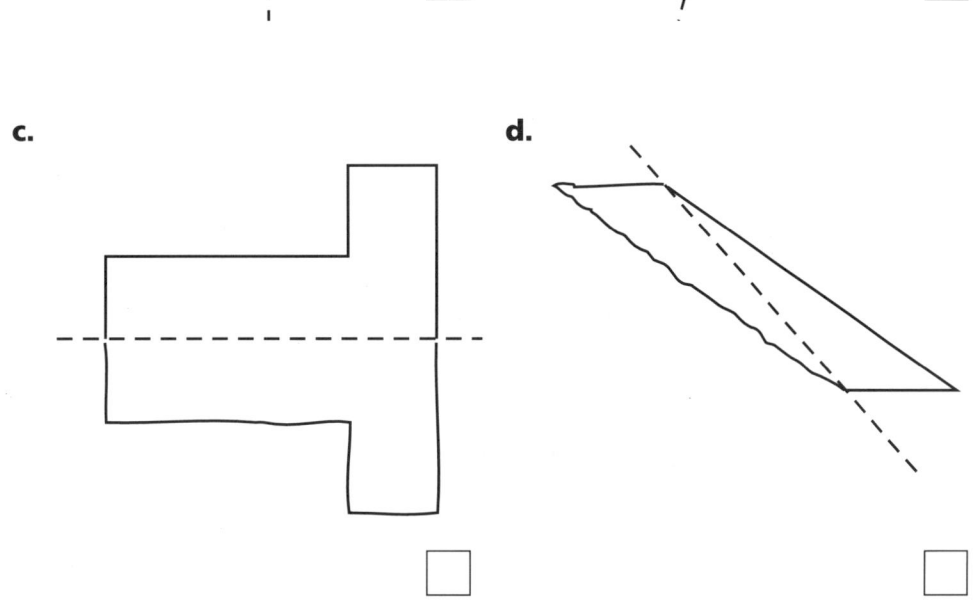

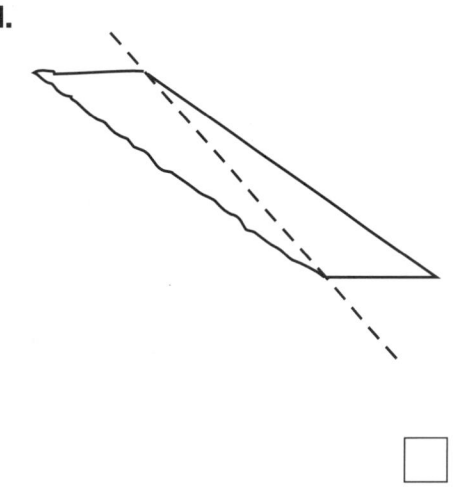

a.

b.

c.

d.

3 Work out how the number in each bottom square has been found and then complete the patterns in the next two boxes.

2	3	1		2	4	3		3	5	2		4	4	5		3	4	
	7				11				17								18	

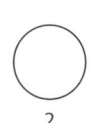

MATHEMATICS: Test 2

1 Costs of videos

E120 — £2.35
E180 — £2.60
E240 — £3.25

a. How much would three E120s cost? _____

b. What would be the cost of one E120 and one E180? _____

c. How much would three E240s cost? _____

2 What fraction of each of these shapes has been shaded in:

a. _____

b. _____

c. _____

d. _____

3 Choose one of these statements to go with each sentence.

likely   **unlikely**   **even**   **certain**

a. A baby will want feeding. _____

b. A bull will run away if you chase it. _____

c. You will need clean socks tomorrow. _____

d. The next person to walk in the door will be female. _____

4 What is the mode of this group: _____

2, 5, 1, 3, 2, 4, 5, 2, 3

MATHEMATICS: Test 2

1 Look at this group of co-ordinates.

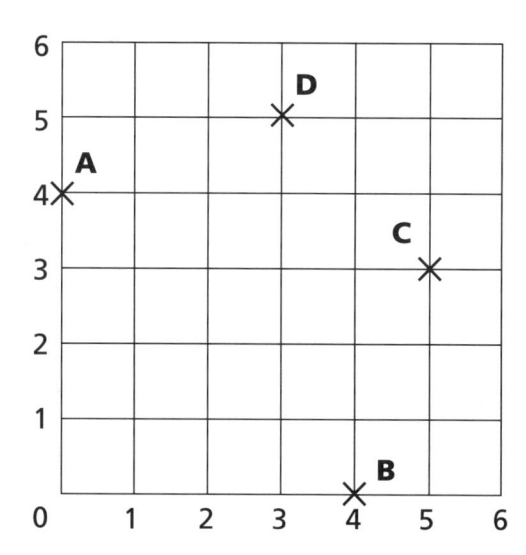

Join up the letters on the left with the co-ordinates on the right.

A	(4, 0)
B	(5, 3)
C	(3, 5)
D	(0, 4)

2 Work out the answers to each of these.

    a. $\frac{2}{5}$ of 20 _____   **b.** 15% of 200 _____

    c. $\frac{2}{3}$ of 27 _____   **d.** 40% of 50 _____

3 Write down the square of each of these numbers:

    4   7   8   9   10

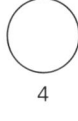

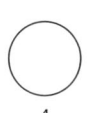

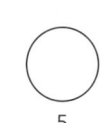

_____   _____   _____   _____   _____

MATHEMATICS: Test 2

1 A dice is thrown 50 times and these are the results of each throw.

2	3	4	1	1	5	6	3	2	4
6	4	3	1	2	4	5	2	3	3
4	4	5	3	2	2	6	6	1	4
4	6	2	6	5	2	5	3	1	5
1	4	6	6	6	4	6	5	3	2

Complete this frequency table to show how often each score comes up. (You may draw on the scores if it helps.)

Score	1	2	3	4	5	6
Frequency						

2 Write either 'sensible' or 'silly' against each sentence.

a. I would use a metre stick to measure my finger. _____

b. I would use a little jug to weigh a brick. _____

c. I would use a metre click wheel to measure a running track. _____

d. I would use a weighing scale to find out if a bag of sugar was heavier than a jar of jam. _____

e. I would use a metre stick to measure the distance between London and Manchester. _____

MATHEMATICS
Test 3

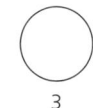

1
  a. 10 children share £150. How much do they each receive?

  b. A piece of material 496 cm long is divided into 100 sections. How long is each section?

  c. A work surface is 5270 mm long. How long is that in metres?

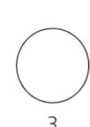

2 Put each list of temperatures in order with the coldest first.

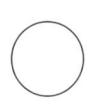

  a. 14°, 20°, –3°, 5°

  b. –6°, –10°, 0°, 8°

  c. 0°, –3°, 3°, –4°

3 Four children start off with these amounts of money:

Asmat – £13.27   **Roy – £12.40**
Ann – £18.00   **Don – £14.05**

They each spend £2.43 on a train ride. How much do they each have left?

Asmat _____ Roy _____ Ann _____ Don _____

4 There are 30 children in a class and 60% are boys. How many are girls?

TOTAL 11

MATHEMATICS: Test 3

1 Work out each division sum and show how you find the answer:

a.
$$34\overline{)9146}$$

b.
$$4116 \div 28$$

2 t = total cost
n = number of items bought
p = price of each item

So t = n × p

a. What will the total cost be if 4 marbles are bought at 15p each?

_____

b. What will the total cost be if 10 lollies are bought at 50p each?

_____

c. If the total cost is £28.00 and 4 items are bought, what is the cost of each item?

_____

d. If the total cost is £200 and each item costs £10, how many items have been bought?

_____

3 The area (A) of a square is found by multiplying the length (L) of one side, by itself or A = L × L. What is the area of a square if its side is 15 cm?

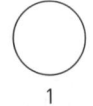

_____

46

MATHEMATICS: Test 3

1 Use the signs = > or < to make each of these sentences true.

   a. A mile is _____ a kilometre

   b. A litre is _____ a gallon

   c. An inch is _____ a centimetre

   d. 10 mm is _____ a centimetre

   e. 1 litre is _____ a pint

   f. 1000 g is _____ a kilogram

2 Draw the net for a square-based pyramid where the sides of the pyramid base are each 4 cm and the faces are equilateral triangles.

MATHEMATICS: Test 3

1 Children in two classes did a survey of their most popular cartoon characters. These pie charts show the results.

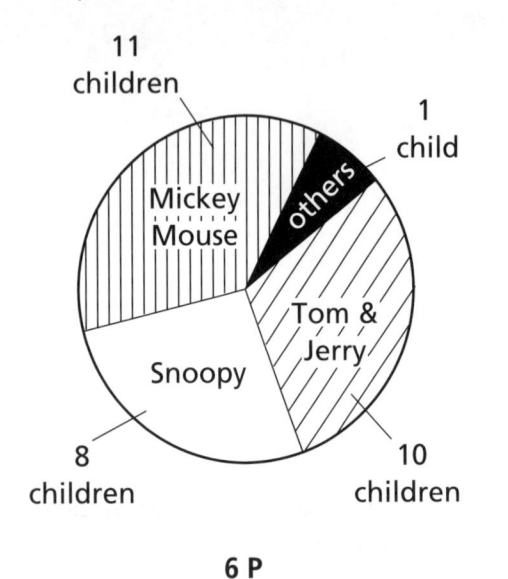

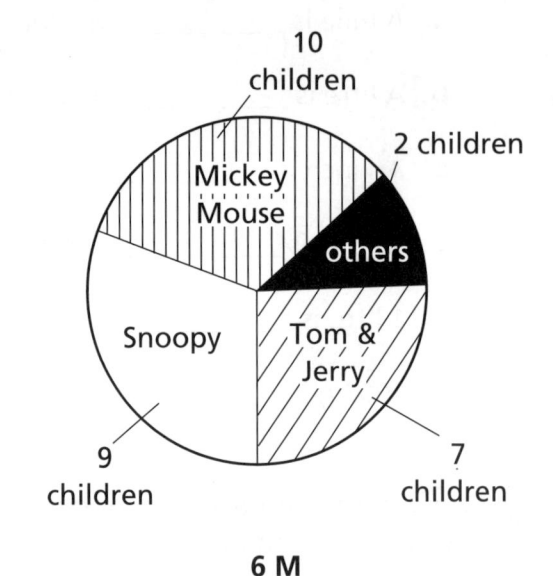

6 P

- 11 children — Mickey Mouse
- 1 child — others
- 10 children — Tom & Jerry
- 8 children — Snoopy

6 M

- 10 children — Mickey Mouse
- 2 children — others
- 7 children — Tom & Jerry
- 9 children — Snoopy

a. How many children are there in each class? _____

b. What percentage of children in 6M liked Tom and Jerry? _____

c. What fraction of children in 6P liked Tom and Jerry? _____

d. Which was the favourite programme in 6P? _____

e. How many votes did Snoopy get altogether? _____

2 a. A lady throws a dice and hopes to get a 6. Mark a cross (✗) on the line, to show the probability of her getting the 6.

impossible   0.5   certain

b. Put a tick (✔) on the line to show the probability of the dice landing on an odd number.

MATHEMATICS: Test 3

1 Put a tick (✔) alongside the sum which gives the answer 4·26.

    a. 3·19   **b.** 6·29   **c.** 1·82   **d.** 3)12·78
       +1·17   −1·03   ×   3

2 Show where you would place each sentence on this probability line:

impossible   fair chance   certain

    A. I'll have to do work at school

    B. My parents will win the lottery this week

    C. I'll ride in a car tomorrow

    D. It will be dark tonight

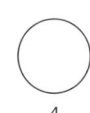

3   **a.** I take 3 away from a number and then divide it by 2. The result is 5. What was the starting number?

       b. I add 4 to a number and then multiply it by itself. The result is 81. What was the starting number?

49

MATHEMATICS
Answers

Test 1

Page 36 **1. a.** 631 **b.** 136

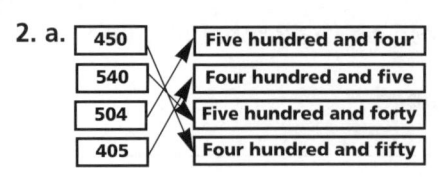

2. a.
- 450 → Five hundred and forty
- 540 → Five hundred and four
- 504 → Four hundred and fifty
- 405 → Four hundred and five

b. 504 **c.** 504 **d.** 504

3. a. 639 **b.** 240
c. two hundred and forty

Page 37 **1.** £7.39
2. a. Murray **b.** Drake **c.** Year 3 **d.** 17
e. 31
3. 100 ÷ 10 = 10, 16 ÷ 2 = 8, 15 ÷ 3 = 5,
45 ÷ 5 = 9, 2 × 6 = 12, 5 × 4 = 20

Page 38 **1. a.** 84p **b.** 48p **c.** 79p
d. 1.04 or 104p

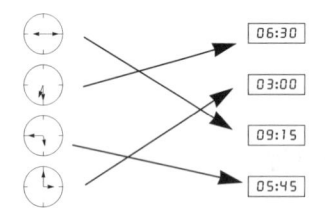

2. a. (clock faces matched to 06:30, 03:00, 09:15, 05:45)

3. a. centimetres **b.** metres
c. centimetres **d.** metres

Page 39 **1. a.** 4 **b.** 7 **c.** 10 **d.** 5
2. With right angles – rectangle, square (triangle)
without right angles – circle, pentagon, hexagon (triangle)
3. a. 6, 5 **b.** square, rhombus (diamond)

Test 2

Page 40 **1. a.** A = 8 piles, 90 left over
B = 14 piles 27 left over
C = 24 piles 6 left over
D = 40 piles 29 left over
2. a. 9 **b.** 7 **c.** 7 **d.** 45
3. a. ✔ **b.** ✘ **c.** ✔
4. a. 8 → 1,2,4,8 **b.** 16, → 1,2,4,8,16
c. 49 → 1,7,49

Page 41 **1. a.** B and C
2. a. ✔ **b.** ✘ **c.** ✔ **d.** ✘
3. a. Multiply the first two numbers on the top row and then add the third to make the number on the bottom. 21 and 6

Page 42 **1. a.** £7.05 **b.** £4.95 **c.** £9.75
2. a. $\frac{3}{4}$ **b.** $\frac{2}{4}$ or $\frac{1}{2}$ **c.** $\frac{1}{4}$ **d.** $\frac{1}{4}$
3. a. certain **b.** unlikely **c.** likely
d. even
4. 2

Page 43 **1.** A → (3,5), B → (5,3), C → (4,0), D → (0,4)
2. a. 8 **b.** 30 **c.** 18 **d.** 20
3. 16, 49, 64, 81, 100

Page 44 **1.**

S	1	2	3	4	5	6
F	6	9	8	10	7	10

2. a. silly **b.** silly **c.** sensible
d. sensible **e.** silly

Test 3

Page 45 **1. a.** £15 **b.** 4.96 cm **c.** 5.27 m
2. a. –3°, 5°, 14°, 20°
b. –10°, –6°, 0°, 8°
c. –4°, –3°, 0°, 3°
3. Asmat – £10.84 Roy – £9.97
Ann – £15.57 Don – £11.62
4. 12

Page 46 **1. a.** 269 **b.** 147 (marks may be given at discretion)
2. a. 60p **b.** 500p or £5.00 **c.** £7.00
d. 20
3. 225

Page 47 **1. a.** > **b.** < **c.** > **d.** = **e.** > **f.** =
2. a. (square with diamond inside)

Page 48 **1. a.** 6P is 30, 6M is 28 **b.** 25% **c.** $\frac{1}{3}$
d. Mickey Mouse **e.** 17
2. (a) × (b) ✔ 0,5

Page 49 **1.** d is correct
2. impossible — B; fair — C; certain — A; D between fair and certain
3. a. 13 **b.** 5

MATHEMATICS: Answers

Conversion of score into National Curriculum Levels

Test 1 (Level 3)	
Level 2 or below	0 – 9
Some work towards Level 3 with many areas to be addressed	10 – 18
Working within Level 2 and towards Level 3	19 – 30
Working well at Level 3	31 – 45

Test 2 (Level 4) and/or Test 3 (Level 5)	
Working below level tested	0 – 15
Some work towards level tested with many areas to be addressed	16 – 27
Working within prior level and towards the level tested	28 – 42
Working well at level tested	43 – 52

SCIENCE
Testing your child's science

What do the National Tests cover?

At Key Stage 2 your child will be studying four areas of science in school. These are:

1. Experimental and investigative science
2. Life processes and living things
3. Materials and their properties
4. Physical processes.

The National Tests cover Life processes and living things, Materials and their properties and Physical processes, with elements of Experimental and investigative science being incorporated where appropriate. Because the science test is shorter than the tests in Maths and English, each test does not cover all the areas of study from the science curriculum, so it is important that your child follows the complete science curriculum in school. However, the practice test printed here gives as comprehensive a coverage as is possible of the science curriculum.

Setting the science tests

The practice test should take your child about 35 minutes to complete. The test is graduated so that questions start at Level 3 and move on to Levels 4 and 5. It might be advisable to let your child start by attempting a section at a time, phasing the whole test over two or three days. In this way, they will be able to give of their best without becoming tired. Whilst each test is designed to be completed in 35 minutes, for practice you could allow about 30 minutes for each section. Eventually, your child can be asked to complete the whole test in the correct time.

Ask your child to carry out the test in silence and to complete it on their own. If there are words they cannot read or do not understand, you can read out these words or phrases to your child particularly specific scientific words, e.g. insulator, predator. Some questions will require scientific words in the answers, e.g. evaporated, gravity. The help given should be confined to reading or writing words rather than explaining their meaning. Your child will need a pencil, a ruler and a rubber to write the answers. Your child should write his/her answers on the line or within the space provided, or tick the appropriate boxes.

Finally, advise your child to read the questions carefully and then answer as many questions as they can. If they cannot answer a question they should move on and come back to it at the end of the test.

A simple marking scheme is provided for every question with a range of acceptable alternative answers.

SCIENCE: Test

Read this carefully

> **Answers**
>
> Write your answer on the lines provided.
>
> For some questions, you may need to draw an answer, for others you simply put a tick or cross in the correct boxes.

> You have 35 minutes to complete this test.

SCIENCE

Test

1 **Flowers**

Here is a drawing showing some parts of a lily flower which has been pulled apart. The name of each part is given.

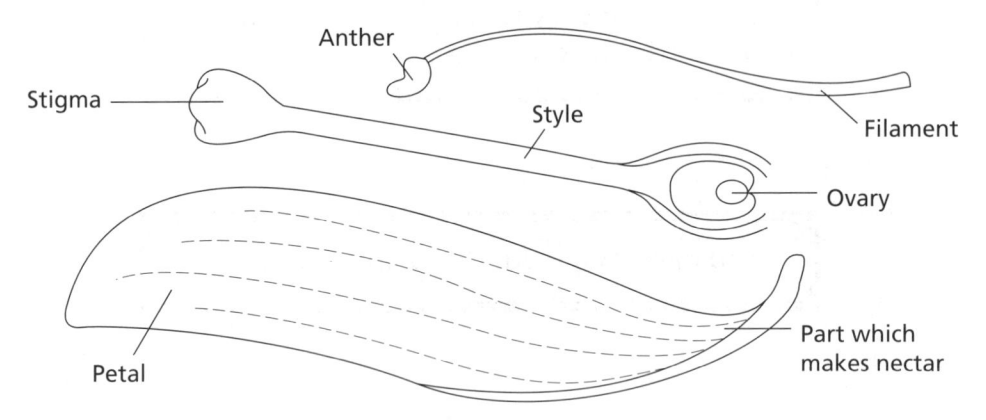

a. Which part produces pollen?
   _____

b. On which part does a visiting insect leave pollen?
   _____

c. Why does a part of the petal make nectar?
   _____

d. Which part of the flower will make the seed?
   _____

2 **Naming flowers**

W   X   Y   Z

SCIENCE: Test

Use this key to find the names of flowers W, X, Y and Z

A Petals all the same size .... Go to B
   Some petals larger than others .... Violet

B Flower has 5 stamens.............................. Primrose
   Flower has more than 5 stamens .... Go to C

C Flower has 1 carpel .... St. John's Wort
   Flower has more than 1 carpel .... Strawberry

Write the letter W, X, Y or Z against the name of the flower

The strawberry is flower _____

The St. John's Wort is flower _____

The primrose is flower _____

The violet is flower _____

3 Smoking and health

Cigarette smoke contains the drug nicotine to which smokers become addicted. It also contains tar which can cause lung cancer and heart disease. On the side of a packet of cigarettes are written the amounts of nicotine and tar. The Government also writes a warning to smokers advising them of the dangers of smoking.

Here are some Government figures:

	Amount of tar in one cigarette (mg)	Amount of nicotine in one cigarette (mg)
Brand A	3	0.3
Brand B	6	0.6
Brand C	9	0.6
Brand D	12	1.1
Brand E	14	0.9

a. Which brand will give the greatest risk of lung cancer?

_____

b. Which brand could be the most addictive?

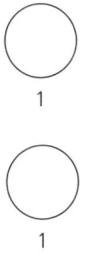

_____

SCIENCE: Test

On the back of Brand B is written:

> Warning by HM Government
> SMOKING DURING PREGNANCY CAN
> SERIOUSLY DAMAGE YOUR BABY'S HEALTH
> AND MAY LEAD TO PREMATURE DEATH

c. What advice would you give to an expectant mother who smokes?

_____

4 Making a cup of tea

a. On this drawing of a glass kettle being used to make a cup of tea, write on the picture the words gas, liquid or solid where you see them.

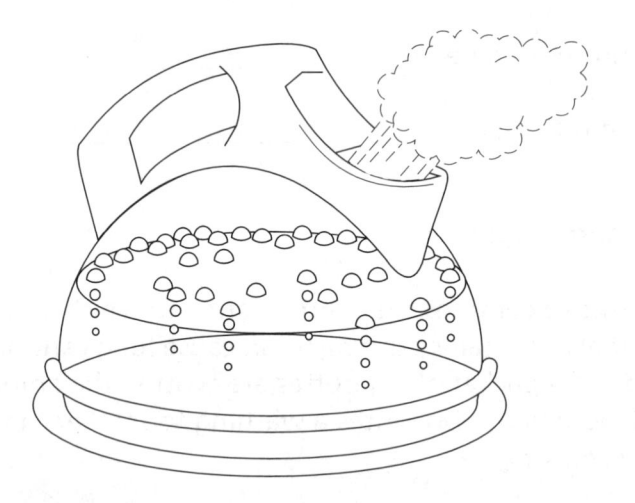

If the hot water is added to a teapot with some tea leaves, you have to use a tea strainer when you pour the tea in a cup. If you use a tea bag, you do not need a strainer.

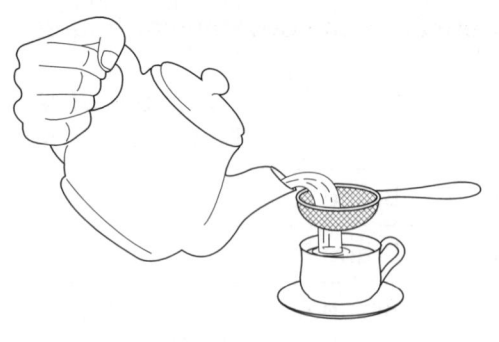

b. Why do you **not** need a strainer when you use a tea bag?

_____

When we put some sugar in the tea, it seems to disappear.

c. What is the scientific word for what happens to the sugar?

_____

SCIENCE: Test

You use a spoon to stir the sugar
into your tea.

    c. Write down why a metal spoon would feel warmer than a plastic one when you stir your tea.

    _____

5 The Moon

There is a full Moon shining. Its position at 8 o'clock in the evening is shown on the picture.

    a. Draw the shadow of the boy on the picture.

    _____

    b. On the picture, draw where the Moon will be seen at 12 o'clock, midnight.

    _____

    c. If the boy came back 14 days later and stood in the same place and at the same time, what would he see?

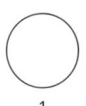

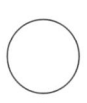

    _____

SCIENCE: Test

d. How long does it take for the Moon to orbit the Earth?

_____

e. The Sun gives out light. It is said to be luminous. The Moon is not luminous.
Explain why we see the Moon as a bright object in the sky.

_____

_____

6 The pond

Here are some living things found in a pond. Their job in the food chain is given.

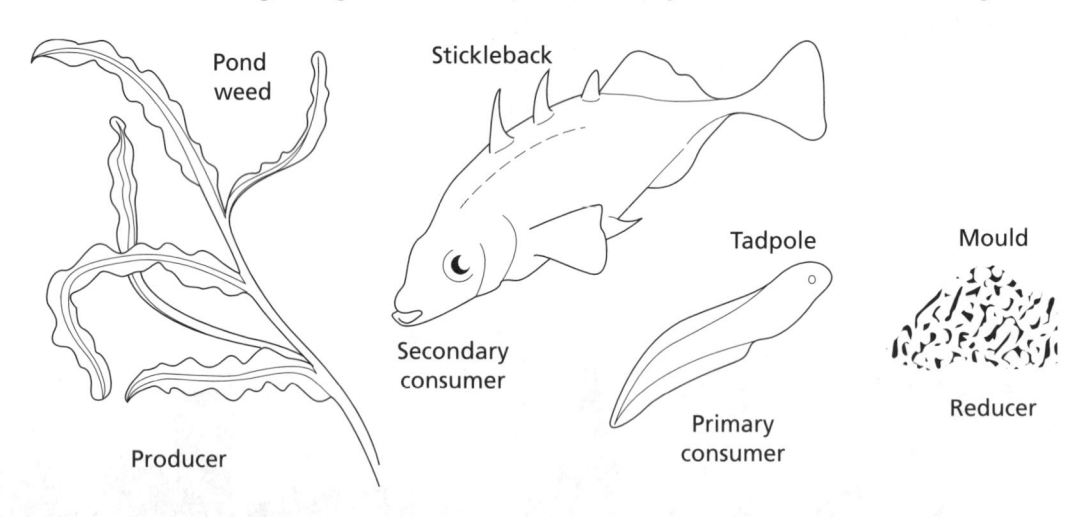

- Pond weed — Producer
- Stickleback — Secondary consumer
- Tadpole — Primary consumer
- Mould — Reducer

a. Draw the food chain that links these living things.

_____

_____

b. How do the producers get their food?

_____

_____

Pond weed, sticklebacks, mould and tadpoles are all living things.

c. What three life processes do all these living things have in common?

_____

_____

SCIENCE: Test

7 **Circuits**

Here are the parts you would use to make a circuit that will light up a bulb. Underneath each drawing is the symbol that is used to draw that part in a circuit.

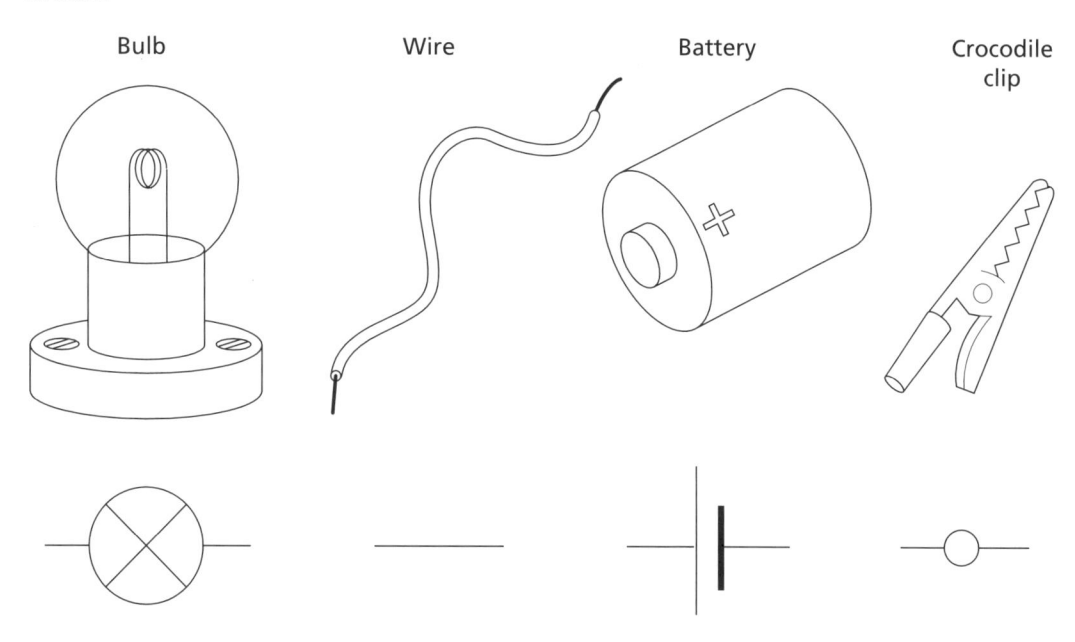

Bulb　　　　　Wire　　　　　Battery　　　　　Crocodile clip

a. Draw a diagram to show how you would put these together to make the bulb light up.

The symbol for a switch is —•⁄•—

b. Draw a second diagram to show where you would put a switch to turn the bulb on and off. Show the switch in the ON position.

TOTAL

SCIENCE: Test

8 Soil

Mark and Jane want to find out which soil is best to use for planting their seeds. Their teacher said that the best soil is one that does not need watering very often.

They took four pots and filled each one with a different soil. They poured on some water and measured how long it took for the water to just start to run out of the hole at the bottom of the pot.

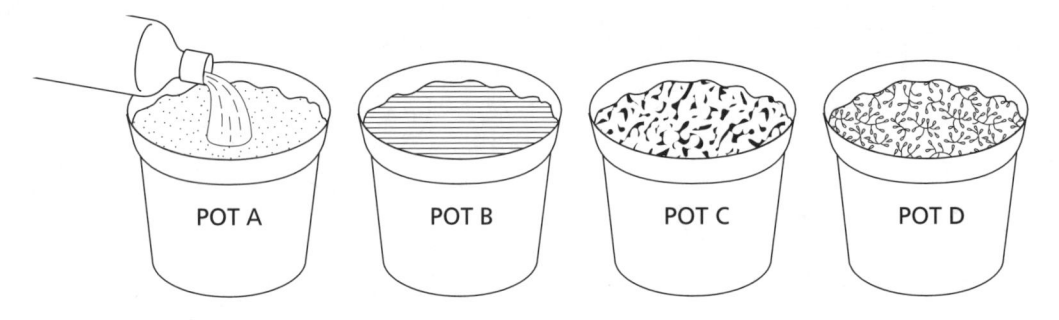

POT A   POT B   POT C   POT D

	Type of soil	Time for water to pass through
POT A	Sand	45 seconds
POT B	Clay	4 minutes 15 seconds
POT C	Peat	2 minutes 30 seconds
POT D	Garden soil	2 minutes

a. Which soil would be the best to use for their seeds?

b. Why do you think this?

c. Write down **two** ways Mark and Jane could make their experiment a fair test.

d. How do plants get the goodness (nutrients) from the soil?

SCIENCE: Test

9 **Straw pipes**

You can make a pipe from a drinking or art straw by flattening the end and cutting it like this. It is played by blowing through the cut end.

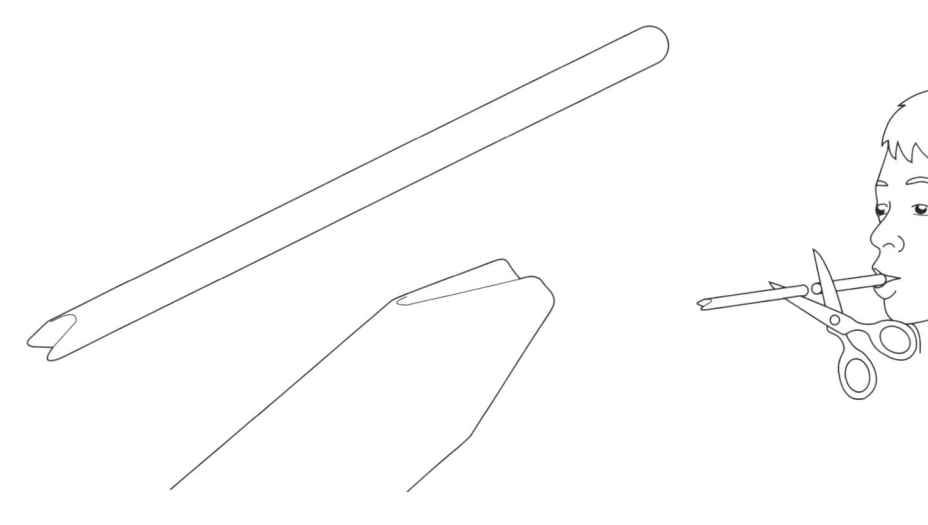

a. Why does the cut end make a sound when it is blown?

_____

b. What will happen if you cut the straw in half and blow again?

_____

c. How could you make the sound louder?

_____

d. Explain how you can hear the straw pipe playing.

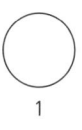

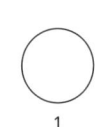

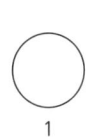

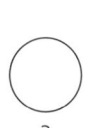

_____

_____

_____

SCIENCE
Answers

1 **a** anther **b** stigma **c** to attract insects **d** ovary

2 strawberry flower = W   St John's Wort = Y   primrose = X   violet = Z

3 **a** Brand E **b** Brand D **c** Stop smoking/do not smoke

4 **a** gas = steam   liquid = water   solid = kettle
   b The tea bag strains/filters it
   c Dissolve(s)
   d Metal is a better conductor than plastic

5 **a** and **b** 
   c He would see a new Moon/no Moon
   d 28 days
   e The light from the Sun is reflected by the surface of the Moon

6 **a** producer → primary consumer → secondary consumer → reducer
   pondweed → tadpole → stickleback → mould
   b They make their own food by photosynthesis/ from carbon dioxide, water and sunlight
   c nutrition/feeding; growth; reproduction

7 **a** Either / or component

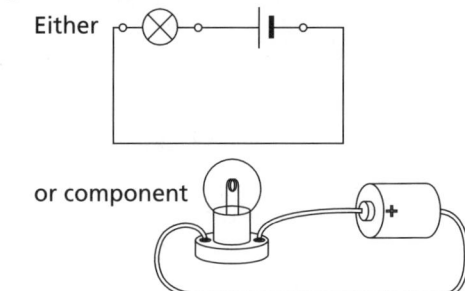

b

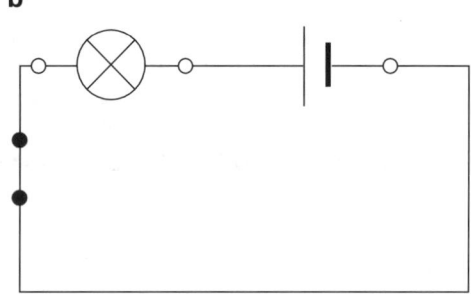

8 **a** Clay/pot B
   b Water takes longest to pass through
   c 1. Use same amount of water
      2. Use same amount of soil
   d Through their roots

9 **a** It/the end vibrates
   b The sound/note becomes higher
   c Blow harder
   d Vibrations make the air vibrate and vibrations travel through the air. Also the ear/ear drum vibrates

Conversion of score into National Curriculum Levels

Your child has not had enough experience of science. Wait until they have more experience then try the test again.	0 – 8
Working towards Level 3	9 – 14
Working at Level 3	15 – 22
Working at Level 4	23 – 31
Working at Level 5	32 – 43